Wild

A play
By Crystal Skillman

Wild was originally commissioned and world premiered by Kid Brooklyn Productions (Evan F. Caccioppoli, Artistic Director) opening 2012 in Chicago at Mary-Arrchie Theatre Company, with the following team:

Nikki	Julia Daubert
Peter	Evan Linder
Bobby	Michael Manocchio
Jordy	Justin Harner
Vin	Jude Hansen
Ted	Adam Schulmerich

Director	Evan F. Caccioppoli
Production Stage Manager	Dina Marie Klahn
Set Designer	Dustin Pettegrew
Lighting Designer	Fred Uebele
Costume Designer	Katherine Meister
Sound Designer	Zan Rosenthal
Dialect Coach	Rachel Rizzuto
Casting Director	Claire Tuft
Photography	Sophia Nahli Allison

Wild premiered in New York 2014 with Sanguine Theater Company at IRT Theater with the following cast and credits:

Nikki	Diana Stahl
Peter	Hunter Canning
Bobby	Jeff Ronan
Jordy	David Armanino
Vin	Lyonel Reneau
Ted	Joshua Levine

Director	Evan F. Caccioppoli
Production Stage Manager	Lauren Stern
Sets/Lights	Jonathan Cottle
Costumes	Holly Rihn
Sound	Grant Jefferson
Violence Design	Jesse Geguzis
Producers	Jillian Robertson, Karly Fischer and Anna Fearheiley

All productions of this play are required to include the following credit on the title page of the program:

Wild received its World Premiere in June 2012 from Kid Brooklyn Productions in Chicago, IL.

CHARACTERS

BOBBY – 24. Wears his heart on his sleeve until he is crossed.

PETER – 25. Bobby's boyfriend. Explosive and highly insecure.

NIKKI – 25. Harsh. Blunt. Vulnerable.

JORDY – 19. Neurotic. Unsure. Destructive.

VIN – 23. Patient, solid – seems to have it all together.

TED – 26. A rock – always there.

TIME
Now.

PLACE
A beach in Chicago.

ACTS & SCENES
ACT ONE:
Scene 1 – "Freezing" (Nikki, Peter)
Scene 2 – "Honesty" (Peter, Bobby)
Scene 3 – "Wounded" (Bobby, Jordy)
Scene 4 – "Reunion" (Jordy, Bobby, Peter)
Scene 5 – "Dinner" (Bobby, Peter)
Scene 6 – "Kindness" (Peter, Vin)
Scene 7 – "Chase" (Ted, Bobby, Jordy)

ACT TWO:
Scene 8 – "Trick" (Bobby, Nikki)
Scene 9 – "Break" (Peter, Ted)
Scene 10 – "This" (Vin, Peter)
Scene 11 – "Message" (Jordy, Bobby, Peter)

Wild

A play by Crystal Skillman

ACT ONE

1. "FREEZING"

Sounds of the beach in darkness. Lights up on a empty beach on Lake Michigan. Night, late April, freezing out. Nikki smokes a cigarette. She is high. She drinks a covered beer. Huddles her jacket around her. Speaks to someone offstage.

NIKKI: BE A FUCKING ADULT! That's what I wanted to scream at them. Fucking kids in the bar. Under age. You know they were. Nineteen year old piss ant shit faced—
Don't. Don't stick up for them because they looked--.
Because they were hot.
With their *(mimics clothes)* and *(mimics faces)*.
Whatever insecure glittery shit is exploding all over your jean-ed ass THEN TAKE THEM THE FUCK OFF YOU TRENDY MOTHERFUCKER.
Because yes – this twenty five year old knows how to act in this fucking "cruel, cruel world."
And if you don't act like who you are – who you really are.
This world will. Eat you. Alive.
I should go home. I shouldn't be here. I will. Go home. I'll-
Thought that the minute you came over, started talking.
The minute you *(imitates a simple gesture/movement Peter did that impressed her).*

I was like "oh really" but wanted to.

You are taking forever. Really? Really? It takes that long to fucking piss.

You can't talk when you do it? That's insane. I talk when I shit all the time. Sometimes I find myself talking in the stall to myself. Other people. Depends on how much I take.

I hate ecstasy. Sucks that's all you had. So nineties, whatever that was.

My mom still only watches, like, Wynona Ryder movies. My mom's boyfriend, Phil: "Nikki, you look just like her" but I think that's just because I shop lift.

Phil. He's retarded. A fucking joke. He's fucking blind as a bat but still shoots off guns in their backyard. He said he used to jerk off to her. Wynona Ryder. Kept pictures of her like under his bed in a shoebox. Now he's like forty seven!

Last class I took – "Deconstructing the Twentieth Century" – University of Chicago – my parents made me take fucking classes while at Joffrey -- because how could I really make it - dancing - right!? "No one dances forever." Your body gives out – like that! –

But in class they put on "Reality Bites" and there's fucking Wynona up there and I just see Phil. *(Imitates jerking off)* I don't have a daddy complex.

Maybe when I was younger.

Saw a guy on facebook I gave head and now it's like – oh Jesus – you see those pictures of assholes you've been with and you're like – wow you are so fat or you're going to clearly die the way you take care of yourself.

Those nineteen year old pricks. Kids. About my fucking cigarettes.

"With all you know you shouldn't be killing your body."
You gotta be kidding me.

Christians. JESUS! I bet they are.

NO ONE HAS THE RIGHT TO TELL ME TO QUIT.

I'm not going to wait here forever.

It's so calm.

The waves.

I fucking love bodies of water.

Lake fucking Michigan.

Peter enters. He touches her, excited, and responds to her simply as she talks.

At least here I get to be in the city. You grow up out of a city and all you want is to be in city. Pack yourself in – closer to people, people, people.
Those kids at the bar – they have no sense of how to move in a space.

Their bodies.

They act like they fuck all the time but people who fuck all the time don't move like that. People who fuck all the time. They move with grace. With commitment. Like – *(She moves up and down Peter's body.)*

When I come here. In the morning. If you go this way.

If you start out your day this way.

And it's not easy.

It's not easy to start any day.

Fucking dog walkers. Joggers. Guys in sunglasses. Yoga classes.

Bitches flexing their bodies with other bitches. Used to be me. Showing just enough. Mid drifts. Even in the fucking cold!

Old guys staring.

Young guys looking at young guys.

Sometimes I run.

Sometimes I run until I fall down.

It's hard to run when you cry but I like it.

I never hurt myself enough.
I like hospitals.

They take care of you.

Once I stayed here all day. I watched the sky change. The sun rise.
It's starting to rain. It's --.
Can you feel that? Can you?
I feel -- .

You ever walk this way before? I have. So many times.

I've met a lot of fucking people.

It's not always the same.

Sometimes-.

Are we staying here?

Or are we going somewhere ... ?

You better have more I need to get HIGH ...

I should go. I should go the fuck home.

PETER: Where's home?

NIKKI: Peter, is that your ...?

PETER: Don't use my name.

She takes off her coat. She takes off her shirt.

NIKKI: I love.
I love it when it's fucking freezing.
Peter.

*As scene transitions, sound is heard: a phone ringing.
Peter's voicemail picks up.*

PETER: You've reached Peter Marks. Leave a message.

Beep.

NIKKI: Peter. I know this is – it's Nikki – from the beach a few months ago. If you're there just --. It's just – I'm -- hello - PETER?

2. "HONESTY"

Lights snap up. Six months later. July, Afternoon. Lights up on the beach. Only this time filled with activity: litter, bags, discarded food. The water laps at the shore. Bobby storms on, carrying tons of bags. He's breathing heavily, uncertain what to do, looks like he's just been emotionally shot. Peter enters quickly after him - still holding his phone. He cautiously approaches Bobby.

BOBBY: Why?

PETER: Honesty.

BOBBY: ...

PETER: You said you wanted honesty, Bobby.

BOBBY: You fucked a woman.

PETER: Yes, but --

BOBBY: You tell me while we're shopping?

PETER: What difference does that make?

BOBBY: Who is she?

PETER: She's a dancer or something.

BOBBY: Oh my god. A stripper.

PETER: No. No. That's what you think I --

BOBBY: What day?

PETER: You were taking the Series 7. I don't know. Let's go home - Be angry just ... whatever you need -- just let me -- It was one night. A mistake. Bobby.

BOBBY: March 21st. After the Gaga concert? You know I know dates. Yes it was - the next day Jerry had like a hypoglycemic reaction.

PETER: A cat isn't a person.

BOBBY: ...?

PETER: You talk about it like it's a person. All you do is talk about the fucking cat.

BOBBY: We have two cats.

PETER: Yeah and they are nasty and they smell and they bite me.

BOBBY: Because they know who you are. They love strangers. Strangers they can trust but you!

PETER: I didn't want to hurt you.

BOBBY: What does she look like?

PETER: I don't even remember.

BOBBY: Liar. What's her name.

PETER: Nikki something. It was months ago.

BOBBY: ...
Where?

PETER: You really want details?

BOBBY: I need to know.

PETER: You wanted to go home. I was wound up. Went to Wonder Bar. You wouldn't come with me.
She made fun of my tie. She wanted a cigarette. We came out. We walked.
We ended up here.

BOBBY: Here. You took her here?

PETER: You asked me to tell you the truth.

BOBBY: Because she just called you! If it doesn't mean anything then did she even --.

PETER: I am trying to be honest with you. I'm trying to be--

BOBBY: *(Overlapping)* You're afraid for your soul --

PETER: I don't even know what you're talking about ---

BOBBY: -- It's eaten up and gone to hell --

PETER: You're the one --

BOBBY: -- Because you have no moral center. No accountability --

PETER: -- obsessed with your brother's wedding, your family --

BOBBY: Because they care --

PETER: -- I care about us --

BOBBY: -- I care.

PETER: You won't even talk to me –

BOBBY: Fuck you!

PETER: Calm down.

BOBBY: Go. Go. Go, go, go, go, go, go, go –

Peter goes.

GOOD!

Bobby crumples a bit. Peter comes back.

PETER: I'm going.

BOBBY: I fucking know.

PETER: I'm gone, I already left. You should be dead or dying from grief.

BOBBY: *(Approaching)* Go fuck *Black Swan* bitch.

Bobby pushes Peter. They kiss passionately. Bobby pulls away.

We barely come out here anymore.

PETER: I didn't tell you because I didn't want you to go.

BOBBY: It wasn't always like this.

PETER: Bobby.

BOBBY: Is she ...

PETER: The only one.

BOBBY: I fell in love with you. Right here. It was right here... Peter.

PETER: Push me, kick me, hurt me. Whatever you need. Please don't go.

In transition light, ringing. Nikki's voicemail picks up:

NIKKI: You have reached 415-856-8437. Please leave a message after the tone.

Beep.

BOBBY: Hello Nikki, whoever. I know you called him today. This is Bobby. The BOYfriend. He's sleeping. I can't-. SPEAK. Stay away. Stay the fuck away.

3. "WOUNDED"

*Three weeks later. Midnight. Lights up on Bobby drinking heartily on the beach. Jordy runs on screaming - he's pretty high – drinking or drugs – [*in the Chicago & NYC* *productions Jack Daniels was used]. Bobby screams with him. It's like a release.*

JORDY: AHHHHH!!!!

BOBBY: AHHHHHH! That was insane.

JORDY: That was fucking crazy. *(Beat.)* AHHHHHH!!!

BOBBY: AHHHH!!!!

JORDY: Did you see her face. That party was sad.

BOBBY: It was pathetic.

Jordy offers. They get more high.

JORDY: She bought herself decorations. "Farewell". "Early Retirement." Who does that when they're let go?

BOBBY: No one needs secretaries anymore.

JORDY: To pick that place.

BOBBY: PIPPINS PUB!

JORDY: PIPPINS PUB!

BOBBY: It was like an Irish wake. With cold burgers and an empty fireplace.

JORDY: It's sad.

BOBBY: She was a good one. She's gone. To Patty.

JORDY: Patty.
Peter wasn't there.

BOBBY: Peter doesn't like emotional gatherings.

JORDY: It is sad. It's scary, right?

BOBBY: What?

JORDY: Life! When you don't know what's going to happen.

BOBBY: I'm not scared.

JORDY: I feel bad we left early.

BOBBY: Why?

JORDY: Leaving everybody there. Leaving Patty there.

BOBBY: She wouldn't leave.

JORDY: She didn't want to leave.

BOBBY: When she goes home she has no one.

JORDY: How can you tell?

BOBBY: Too old to be staying out that late with no one.

JORDY: She's like forty.

BOBBY: Old.

JORDY: Old.

BOBBY: Why?

JORDY: I'm always afraid someone's going to throw me in.

BOBBY: Really.

JORDY: Everyone knew I couldn't swim. But Tom fucking Haley. Always fucking throwing me into pools in high school.

BOBBY: Where was that again? Minneapolis?

JORDY: Kansas.

BOBBY: Wow.

JORDY: It's not impressive.

BOBBY: It is.

JORDY: I like watching you.
I like watching you work.

BOBBY: You should watch Peter – you'll get ahead faster.

JORDY: He's predicable – there's no point. I know the outcome of every stock he'll pick.
Green Mountain Coffee! I mean c'mon!
You. You mix it up.

BOBBY: I do?

JORDY: You're inventive. You look ahead. That's a gift, a --.

I get scared shitless just answering the phone. Have all these things I want to say in my head but I don't want to make a mistake. I get so mad when I make a mistake.

BOBBY: I'd like to see you mad.

JORDY: That's fucked up.

BOBBY: You really watch me.

JORDY: I'm there to learn.

BOBBY: Right.

JORDY: You do this thing with your *(imitates Bobby's hair tugging)*.

BOBBY: No.

JORDY: Yeah. It's cute.

BOBBY: You whisper to yourself. In the hallway.

JORDY: To psych myself up. All I'm getting is shit in there.

BOBBY: We all are.

JORDY: I studied like hell. My SATs.

BOBBY: Right.

JORDY: I'm smart – really fucking smart.

BOBBY: Yeah I --

JORDY: I'm pretty sure they're going to fire me.

BOBBY: Jordy --

JORDY: I put out coffee in the North Conference Room - where they brought in Patty - hear them deciding who is on their firing list – the names -

BOBBY: You're an intern.

JORDY: Today! And then there's another internship next year! And finishing college! And I'm supposed to know what I want to do Bobby! And I have no idea what I'm looking for! Not a clue! Wherever I walk into -- Pippin's sweating my balls off - anywhere – I walk in and it's packed and I can barely move with people but I'm looking for someone like me. Someone like me right but everyone I look at they know what the fuck they want to do, where they want to go. And where do I go? Go to a club – Angels and Kings or Downtown Bar and even then, even with everyone trying to go home with someone there's some kind of drive – some kind of –

BOBBY: Passion?

JORDY: I don't know what to do with mine. And I go home with someone. I always go home with someone. Girls, guys, I don't give a fuck. I'm fucking someone and I don't even know I'm there.

BOBBY: Ask yourself who you're fucking. Who they are.

JORDY: If I did that I'd never fuck.

BOBBY: Maybe we should go back to the party.

Bobby starts to go.

JORDY: The first time .... like I'd go to a Jay Haw
thinking that would be ...?

BOBBY: ...

JORDY: Hawks are football. Kansas.

BOBBY: Cheerleader? Jock?

JORDY: I've been with plenty of girls.

Beat.

BOBBY: Your first?

JORDY: He was just a friend of my dad's. Professor.
Emailed me - just me - had an extra ticket. Even getting
ready I'm like what am I doing with this guy? Thin like a
rail. A rake. Like only late twenties but what am I fifteen?
He called me Rabbit I have no idea what the fuck why - I
look scared he says and I am - I'm always scared but I'm not
- we're like just walking back to the fucking car and he pulls
me right behind this wall and just -- just kissing -- like --
like --.

Everyone drinking bud and putting away fucking hot dogs
and burgers and nacho trays from some tail gate party
bullshit - fat ladies with helmet hair just waiting for their
men to get back in their vans, pouring their bodies in but
when we got into the car, when we went to his house, when
we were there, we were there it was like, felt ...

BOBBY: Yeah?

JRDY: You believe in love?

BOBBY: ...

JORDY: Peter - today - pissed I got back late. He gave me a lot of shit. "You want to know how to keep fucking this up Joe? Keep coming back late Joe - "

BOBBY: Why does he call you Joe?

JORDY: He says Jordy is a girls' name.

BOBBY: Peter says shit all the time.

JORDY: Peter - he's all over you. I mean you were always ... but the past few weeks. All he does is stop by asking how you're doing.

BOBBY: You watch a lot.

JORDY: Everyone does.

BOBBY: Then they should mind their fucking business.

JORDY: I just think it's cool how you started at Mesirow at the same time.

BOBBY: Why? Why do you care?

JORDY: You don't want anyone in the office to know.

BOBBY: I don't like to complicate things. We all get shit in there. So, Mesirow isn't a place where I express myself fully, no.

JORDY: What about with me?

BOBBY: ...

JORDY: We should go back. The party.

Jordy gets up to go. Bobby gently grabs his arm.

BOBBY: Northwestern. First day. Sophomore year. Peter walks in right past my desk, could hear on the floor - dress shoes - who dresses up for Econometrics? Slumps in the back. Came up after, he was hungry, I was hungry. We left. It wasn't like there was time or I could see anyone else passing by. I could only hear him - so many questions. "Why, why, why ..." He asked about everything - my family, he told me about his own ... I said he could have mine. That I would be his -. We are together, we live together yes.

JORDY: Does he like to come here?

BOBBY: I like to come here.

JORDY: When was the last time you were here?

BOBBY: I really have to go.

JORDY: Why?

BOBBY: Why the hell do you care Jordy?

JORDY: Because I care about the people I want to fuck.

Beat.

BOBBY: Peter and I are fine. There have been some

complications - there are always complications but we are fine Jordy.

JORDY: Ok.

Jordy sits, starts to put his shoes back on.

BOBBY: We live -- right there (*looks out at their apartment*) - right there with the lights on- and for three weeks since ... since we were last here ... since he told me he was with someone else we say everything's okay, we act like everything's okay, we walk around like ghosts. I don't want to talk about it.

JORDY: He misses you.

BOBBY: How would you know that?

JORDY: The way he watches you.

Bobby kisses Jordy.

JORDY: What happens now?

BOBBY: We don't ask questions. We don't talk. We don't fucking talk about it.

They keep making out.

JORDY: I feel crazy.

BOBBY: Be crazy.

Bobby keeps kissing him, undressing him.

JORDY: Pippin's - on my way to the bathroom - opened the door - looking up in the mirror at my face.
I took my hand. Felt my fist. Punched it. Shards of glass. You should have seen the waiter when I came out. Just putting a kitchen towel around my hand and everything red like fireworks. And for that moment I felt something. Look at me, I'm a wounded motherfucker.

Bobby has stopped kissing him. He undoes the wrapping around Jordy's hand. He kisses the wound.

JORDY: Why me? Why now? Is this because of Peter? You don't want him anymore.

BOBBY: Tell me – tell me: I need this. You don't know how much I fucking need this.

JORDY: You don't know how much I fucking need this.

BOBBY: Louder.

JORDY: You don't know how much I fucking need this! You don't know how much I fucking need this!

Jordy starts taking off his clothes, then takes off Bobby's. They turn to each other.

BOBBY: I'm not going to throw you in.

JORDY: I don't want you to.

BOBBY: You really can't swim?

JORDY: ...

BOBBY: This is. This is fucking crazy.

JORDY: Yes.

Bobby grabs Jordy, touches him passionately, breaks away.

BOBBY: AHHH!!

JORDY: AHHH!!

They run into the water.

4. "REUNION"

Later that night, around 3 AM. In dimly lit darkness, Bobby and Jordy reenter kissing. They dress each other. Jordy leaves. Bobby watches him go. Then Bobby walks up and down, looks out over the waves. He is alone. Grabs his shoes, turns to go home. He looks up at where he lives. Stops. Drops the shoes down. He takes out his phone, dials Peter.

BOBBY: Where are you? Come down. Ok.

Bobby hangs up. Is this the answer? Can he really make things ok now? He looks like he's about to cry. He is breathing heavily. Sinks to his knees on the sand. He can do this, he can do this. He looks out at the waves, whispers to himself.

BOBBY: Try.
Try.
Try.

Bobby digs into the sand. Picks some up. Holds it in his hands. He releases the sand, letting it fall.

Let go.

Bobby still breaths a little heavy, still unsure. Peter arrives.

PETER: Bobby ...?

Bobby is quickly on him. It is real, honest and full of fire. Peter is surprised, but holds him. Peter whispering in his ear:

Where have you ...?

BOBBY: *(While kissing and talking)* I miss you.

Peter kisses him. Bobby pulls Peter to him. Bobby looks around ... this place is not the same. It can't be here. He puts out his hand. Peter takes it. Bobby leads him off.

5. "DINNER"

In transition, sound of ringing. Bobby's voicemail picks up.

BOBBY: Hello you've reached Robert (Bobby) Lahman, Junior Client Reporting Associate at Mesirow Financial. Please leave a message after the beep and I'll get back to you as soon as I can.

Beep.

JORDY: Last night was – AHHHHHHHH! Bobby! Right, it's, it's so good. So good!

That night. Peter comes in after work with a backpack. He sits on the bench. He puts out his iPhone and attaches speakers. He hits play. He smiles when he hears the song. Might do a little dance as he starts putting out a blanket. He unzips the backpack, putting out plates and containers of food. He looks at it all, proud. Goes back to his backpack. Takes out a cool shirt. He undoes his tie, takes off his collared shirt and puts on the cool shirt. Shoves his work clothes in the backpack. He combs his hair. Looks at his reflection in one of the glasses on the blanket. He looks good! He sits. He tries to be good, but can't resist. He starts to snack. He might jump up and dance to the music. Tossing almonds up in the air, catching them. Bobby comes in, unseen, he watches Peter for a minute, taking this in. Bobby sneaks up on him, grabs him. Peter gestures to the goodies that surround them.

PETER: Ta da!

BOBBY: What's this?

PETER: I made dinner!

BOBBY: Sandwiches.

PETER: Hot Sandwiches! All Bobby's favorites. Pickled beets. And Okra. And salad. With all kinds of cheese you like. Goat. Feta. Gouda! Green Grocer Gazpacho!

BOBBY: *(Playfully)* Hmm ... I'm into meat now actually. Steak. Buffalo. Elk.

PETER: Elk.

BOBBY: Anything you catch. Anything you catch and hold with your bare hands I like it.
Rare.

PETER: You were in rare form last night.

BOBBY: Was I?

PETER: You were. Crazy.

BOBBY: You are. Mmmm. Did you put this together in the kitchen?

PETER: Why?

BOBBY: *(sing-song-y/playful)* There's roaches in the kitchen.

PETER: I didn't see anything.

BOBBY: The condo people must have forgotten to spray because I saw one this morning. A little one. It was cute. A baby all alone and then a bigger one came out and they like frolicked all over the kitchen counter like it was a public pool -- so if you put this together there a roach could be in it and come out and crawl up and eat your pretty face!

PETER: Yeah? You like my pretty face huh.

BOBBY: *(Smiling)* Yeah.

PETER: Uh-huh.

Bobby kisses Peter.

BOBBY: What's in the bag?

PETER: Gifts.

BOBBY: Gifts?

Peter holds up Pinot, pours the wine. Bobby goes over to him, takes it. They toast!

PETER: What?

BOBBY: I don't know you look ...

PETER: What?

BOBBY: You haven't worn this since ...

PETER: Hah! See! *(Peter grabs his stomach and thrusts it out)* Five years hasn't made a difference.

BOBBY: *(Patting Peter's small belly, smiling.)* Nooooo.

PETER: Exactly the same.

BOBBY: Exactly.

PETER: You don't like it.

BOBBY: I like it.

PETER: I wanted to look nice for you. What?

BOBBY: Nothing. I just like - the way you're sitting.

PETER: I like the way you're eating. That little grunt noise you make when you like something.

BOBBY: C'mon.

PETER: I love how you give me shit.

BOBBY: Yeah? I love how you are always pacing.

PETER: Only when I'm waiting for you.

BOBBY: Like a caged animal.

Peter acts like an animal. Bobby laughs.

PETER: You. You missed me these past few weeks...

Bobby has a moment of goofiness. The old Bobby. Sticks out his tongue at Peter, then grabs his arm, squeezes.

BOBBY: I missed you.

PETER: I'm lucky.

BOBBY: It's like it never happened. The slate is clean.

PETER: Okay.

BOBBY: *(Eating)* This is good.

PETER: Last night. It hasn't been that good in so --

BOBBY: /Okay.

PETER: Not that /it hasn't --

BOBBY: /No, no.

PETER: -- I just did. I missed --

BOBBY: *(Eating another bite)* Yeah? This is so good.

PETER: Fucking Joe staring at me all day. You see that? Not a word, just (*imitates Jordy's stare*). That fucking kid...

BOBBY: Jordy's ... nice... maybe he needs that - a little kindness.

PETER: Well if he wants something he should say it.

Peter kisses Bobby. Bobby smiles, distracted. Peter gets some gazpacho.

Oh god did I forget the spoons? Have you seen the spoons?

Peter tuns to see Bobby eating with a spoon. Peter takes it from his hand.

PETER: Spoons!

Gives Bobby a playful wack on the head with it.

You are spacey.

BOBBY: I didn't sleep much.

Beat. Bobby looks at Peter. He wants to tell him the truth about the other night, but is silent.

PETER: What?

BOBBY: Nothing.

PETER: You look scared.

BOBBY: No ... I'm just happy we're ...

PETER: You're right this is so good!

BOBBY: It is... *(remembering something)*. Oh! Oh! Oh! *(Laughing)* Ted!

PETER: Ted!

BOBBY: Ted... the wedding! Ted calls crazed - about the rings. So I tell him to go to Steve Quicks - and he goes but the location he goes to is closed and he is crazed freaking out - calls up - "What do I do? Cheryl is going to kill me - this is what I've got to do on the list today" ---

PETER: Cheryl. She is on the war path.

BOBBY: She wants things to be right.

Peter points to the ring on his finger.

PETER: The lady who was helping us - ah! She was like 50 with that scarf - aren't you two the cutest things??! We could make it official.

BOBBY: *(Smiling)* Okay.

PETER: You look surprised.

BOBBY: I just didn't expect ... this ...

PETER: I'm serious ...

BOBBY: Maybe we shouldn't talk about it.

PETER: Ellen called.

BOBBY: What did your lovely sister have to say?

PETER: Nothing. We don't need to talk about it.

BOBBY: What's going on with your dad. C'mon.

PETER: I'm not going to let them worry me anymore.

BOBBY: C'mon he's your -- you have to talk to me about this stuff. You have to talk to someone.

PETER: I am!

BOBBY: I know. Peter...

PETER: Maybe this is a little fast.

BOBBY: No I like fast. I like to move on, get shit done. I can let go.

Neither knows what to say. They eat. Peter skips ahead on the mix. A current pop song comes on. It's peppy!

BOBBY: God.

PETER: You love this song.

BOBBY: I do.

The music plays on. Peter holds Bobby who rests on him.

PETER: I was afraid you were avoiding me. But last night --

BOBBY: It was different.

PETER: Wonderful. Waking up together. You being here with me... I feel so...

BOBBY: You...

PETER: I love you.

A beat. Bobby is leaning on Peter as they look out. Peter can't see Bobby is starting to cry.

Bobby?

BOBBY: The waves. Why we first came here. I was remembering ...

PETER: Bobby, always remembering.

Beat. Bobby looks up at Peter who still holds him.

BOBBY: *(Quietly)* I wasn't acting like I was avoiding you. These past few weeks, I have a specific method of avoiding you. I hear your footsteps, where you go, wherever you are going, I go the opposite. I love you. I do Peter.

PETER: That's it. That's us. Honesty.

BOBBY: Last night. I touched you and you jumped like you were waiting for it – your cock did. And I loved it.

PETER: Yes.

BOBBY: I'm sorry.

PETER: Why are you sorry?

BOBBY: ...

PETER: Bobby.

Bobby turns to face Peter. He takes Peter's hands.

BOBBY: Having an affair is a test of love. How you live with
this tells you everything.
I fucked Jordy. "Joe."
I fucked him here.
He left. And you and I went home. We...

PETER: Why?

BOBBY: Nikki. I've never seen her but I see - I see her face
everywhere I go.

*Peter can't speak. He can't look Bobby in the eye. He
quickly starts grabbing everything he just put out, throwing
it into his bag.*

BOBBY: No no no no don't - please. Don't go. We'll stay
together. We'll work it out ---

PETER: How?

BOBBY: I'll fuck whoever I want and you'll fuck whoever
you want. That's love isn't it?

Transition, ringing. Peter's sister, Ellen, picks up.

ELLEN: *(Quickly)* Peter - we have nothing to talk about -
Dad doesn't want to see you - no -don't call me again - done
-bye.

Sound of hang up. Lights up on Peter screaming into his phone.

PETER: Ellen! You do not hang up on me. Don't fucking hang up on me. Don't hang up. He's our dad, ok ours, if he's this bad, I will visit him, I will fucking be there.

6. "KINDNESS"

Afternoon. Lights up on Peter slamming his phone shut. A fit man emerges from the water, dripping wet, just in his small suit. This is Vin.

VIN: Hey.

PETER: Hey.

VIN: You're sitting on my towel.

PETER: Oh Jesus this is your – Sorry – I'm not - I didn't notice. It's been –

VIN: It's ok.

Vin towels off. He undresses from his swimsuit and dresses into shorts right there as Peter reacts.

PETER: Yeah, -- ok, ok.

VIN: Do you mind if I...?

PETER: No.

VIN: I'm not bothering you.

PETER: Sure. I'm just. No, no.

VIN: Ok.

Vin lies down. Faces sun, attaches speakers to an ipod.
Plays some music.

It's really -- not bothering you.

PETER: I'm only here a few more --. Lunch.

Vin takes out a book and an apple. Starts to read. Peter just
stares at him. Vin glances over.

VIN: That's your lunch? An energy drink?

PETER: Why?

VIN: I might have another apple if you want --

PETER: You always offer food to strangers.

VIN: If they don't move away and stay staring at me maybe
yes. It's a good apple. Farmer's market.
They call it Piñata.

PETER: Piñata. What's that?

VIN: Names they give all those organic apples. This one is
Piñata. Supposed to taste crispy.

Peter refuses the apple. Vin bites. Peter swigs his drink. The
waves. Silence. Vin eyes Peter who seems unable to focus.
Peter peers at the book.

BOBBY: Jordy. We will be one day.

JORDY: What?

BOBBY: Forty.

JORDY: I hope not.

BOBBY: What happened to your hand?

JORDY: It's stupid.

BOBBY: Okay.

Bobby laughs.

JORDY: What?

BOBBY: I don't know.

JORDY: Hot.

BOBBY: So fucking hot.

JORDY: It was so hot today. I was sweating balls going out for lunch. Just walked around, sweat pouring off me.

BOBBY: Yeah?

JORDY: Yeah.

BOBBY: It's cooler over here.

JORDY: I don't like being that close to the water.

VIN: You read it before?

PETER: No.

VIN: Russian Lit.

PETER: I can't.

VIN: That's tough, school system is worse than I thought.

PETER: I don't have time. To read Russian novels.

VIN: Ah. I get it. *(Gesturing to himself)* Grad student. Starting in the fall.

PETER: Cool.

VIN: Came out to spend the summer. And now my parents - are in visiting. To "get to know the city!" Left them practically hitting their heads on the ceiling of my responsibly priced studio apartment. They've never had to spend so much time so close together. So ... I escaped. Shush. Don't tell.

PETER: Who am I going to tell?

VIN: Vin.

PETER: I don't need to know your name Vin and you don't need to know mine I just came here for ten fucking seconds to just – to think ok.

Vin starts to gather his things.

I'm sorry, I --

Wait, just – you shouldn't move. I am leaving, I am, okay?

Vin sits. Peter looks out at the water. A sad look crosses his face.

VIN: You should go out for a swim.

PETER: We live over there.

VIN: We?

PETER: My partner Bobby and I -. You're very – you're very open with strangers.

VIN: I'm kind. Aren't you?

PETER: (*No, no, no*) actually. I'm a son of a bitch. But don't worry I'll –

VIN: You need to sit your ass down.

PETER: Excuse me?

VIN: I don't know you but I think you're having a bad day. I think you're having a really, really bad day and I think before you go back to work and let everyone see you like that - you should sit and not move and just shut the fuck up and look at the waves, and get your shit together, ok?

PETER: This is kindness?

VIN: This is kindness.

Peter sits beside Vin.

PETER: Peter. Mesirow Financial.

VIN: Vin. Northwestern. Mesirow? So you make money and I'm in school just giving it away. Good to meet you.

PETER: No shaking hands okay?

VIN: You do that all day. Gotcha.

PETER: I went to Northwestern.

VIN: Good for you.

PETER: I'm trying to be nice.

VIN: You can keep trying.

PETER: What are you studying?

VIN: Literature.
Anthropology.
Digital Photography of the Modern Age.
Black and White Classical Photography.
Tap.
Just joking.
Modern Dance.
That's this semester. Next semester:
Painting with Sound.
Rhetoric in Marxist Literature.
Homoerotic Studies in Film Noir.

PETER: So you don't give a shit about finding a job.

VIN: I don't care what people say, I live my life.

PETER: And read Russian novels.

VIN: I fucking love Russian novels.

PETER: Who pays for all that?

VIN: Are we really getting into family?

Peter smiles. Vin smiles.

I go swimming to forget about that.

PETER: So what do you think about out there?

Vin gestures to the waves.

Right! The waves and shit.

VIN: Yeah, the waves, the sky.

PETER: Sun.

VIN: I like it better when it rains.

PETER: Why?

VIN: You dive underneath, you feel it coming down. It's nice. Warm.

PETER: Yeah. Right, yes, well. This was ...

VIN: Next time go out for a swim.

PETER: I don't want to. I don't meet people here at midnight to do shit like that so.

VIN: I don't...

PETER: What do you think of the name Jordy?

VIN: Sounds like a girls' name.

PETER: Fucking right. Right! Do you know what I mean?!

VIN: Okay, okay, okay, okay. It's okay.

Vin sits cross legged and breaths, getting Peter to imitate him until Peter breaks.

PETER: Oh my god how are you so patient?

VIN: I just – I accept.

PETER: Wow that's really. Zen master.

VIN: You know, it's easier to tell a stranger why.

PETER: Why what?

VIN: Why you act pissed but look like you're going to cry.

PETER: My father. He's sick. He's really fucking sick. Sure you can say it's prostate cancer but it's not even just one thing – drinking like – and his body is literally falling apart. Has been. Piece by piece. Not that he gives a shit. When I brought Bobby home? I didn't prepare them. We just walked in. As if we could walk in and everything would be ok. Bobby's just like, "They're shit, forget them!" Bobby's family they're – they love him. Bobby's mom and dad, his brother Ted rally around him like –and mine? My sister Ellen tells me I'm going to hell. She doesn't say those words but she leaves reports of misery on my phone. Sends photos of dear old dying dad. Today's message? "He's in the ER now - hope you're happy." So I fucking have patience. I get it together. I take my lunch break. I go to the hospital. I can't get past the doors.

All the other people going in and out -- here's the thing - if you asked my family to cut me up and said to my fucked up dying father what part of your son do you like? What one fucking thing of your son – what redeeming quality do you love? He wouldn't pick any part of me.

They wouldn't pick any part of me. I hurt them because of who I am. I hurt Bobby - I fucked someone else. A woman. I don't know why. I fucked it up. And I'm telling you this because I hurt people and I don't know why. I can't change what I did and I can't fix it. I'm just trying and it's not good enough. Not any piece of me is good enough and I don't know what to do.

VIN: What's in the drink?

PETER: Vodka.

VIN: Russians drink to sadness. They accept where they live. You can do other things.

PETER: Other things?

VIN: I'm starting yoga here. Fridays.

Peter hands Vin a card.

PETER: If you need to make an investment.

VIN: I'm okay for now. That's really nice of you.

PETER: I love the way you talk.

VIN: Thanks.

PETER: So.

VIN: So.

PETER: Vin. Yoga.

VIN: Yoga.

PETER: Fridays.
I think you're beautiful Vin. I think you're really fucking beautiful and I just wanted to say that.
I don't do yoga because I hate cramping but thanks.

Peter gets up, grabs his drink, turns to go.

VIN: You: if I only had ten seconds?
I like your mouth.
Your eyes.
Your hair.
Your middle.
Your ass. Your arms.
Every part of you.
I'm sorry about your dad.

Transition light: Ted, live, on the beach, talking on the phone.

TED: Bobby. I thought you were coming this morning to go over - Ah! I see you! Right! You see me? *(He waves.)* You see me? See me? I'm waving!

7. "CHASE"

Lights fully up on Bobby and Ted on the beach. After work, overcast.

TED: -- Because we have too many fucking pillows! Right, Bobby am I right?

BOBBY: Way too many fucking pillows.

TED: I mean she cannot go into Crate and Barrel. And Bed, Bath, Beyond – forget it! She likes them in certain places, places each pillow in certain Feng Shui positions– like she knows what that is. Like you'd enter our apartment before not sure what to think of – testing our friendship - and go "well I don't know about these assholes" and then see a red pillow with fringe – and be like well now – now: "I love these people. I think so highly of them, I'm never going to leave." Because of pillows! With cat faces printed on them! I swear to god she loves pillows with cats –

BOBBY: She loves cats.

TED: That woman loves cats.

BOBBY: I love cats.

TED: Who doesn't love cats? You move a pillow – out of place – Cheryl's eyes (*he imitates*) – like they're going to pop – like that guy they brought in to ER when his eye was hanging out I showed you on my phone?

BOBBY: Oh that was so gross.

TED: Gross right! I mean you open a door to our house and they're just spilling out. Pillows! Cats!

Dash isn't even like that about toys. Dash. If he was here right now he would be mauling that seagull. He loves nature.

BOBBY: He likes first grade?

TED: Does he?! You should see his paintings! Oh my god. I'm afraid they'll put us in jail because they do seem kind of dark to me – weird but they're great. He made you one.

BOBBY: Wow -- he likes fire.

TED: They have a lot of red paint.

BOBBY: Dad of the Year.

TED: Usually Peter calls me that.

BOBBY: Yeah.

TED: Mom has been asking when you're going to come by. Get this she made you guys wind chimes – you know how she's into that now – they're great but Cheryl – not her thing.

BOBBY: This is a great place for the wedding right? Perfect.

TED: Yeah it's gotta be perfect you know how Cheryl is.

BOBBY: I do.

TED: You don't keep up your end as Best Man and she'll make me replace your ass. There's already the Godfather situation.

BOBBY: That is not my fault!

TED: The priest needed to know you were going to be there!

BOBBY: My cell phone died!

TED: Well, Cheryl panicked. Now we're stuck with Uncle Mickey as Godfather forever. And he can't even remember his own name.

BOBBY: I'm not going to fuck it up. I won't let you down. Okay – bro.

Bobby does a goofy fist bump to Ted.

TED: *(Grinning)* Idiot.

BOBBY: I am going to be the best best man. So – duties.

TED: Making sure that I don't look hung over. That I don't throw up. The ring.

BOBBY: And I'll be right here – this is great. With the water.

TED: You've thought about this a lot.

Beat - this is true.

BOBBY: Vows here by the rocks I think.

TED: I like it.

BOBBY: We could be here. Cheryl can come up over there.

TED: Cheryl will love that. She loves entrances. You should see her dress it's like a ball of tulle. You can barely see her face.

BOBBY: You're not supposed to see the dress.

TED: Bobby we've been together since I was eighteen. I knocked her up with Dash. I see -- everything!

BOBBY: Right.

TED: Married! I don't see why we have to do this now but Cheryl: "What is Dash going to say when he's grown up about his parents - out of wedlock." I swear to god it's just because she watches those Wedding reality shows –

BOBBY: Ted, Peter and I –

TED: You guys. You guys always fight.

BOBBY: It's been a crazy time.

TED: What do you mean?

BOBBY: I really don't want to talk about it.

TED: He's coming to the wedding.

BOBBY: ...

TED: Did you tell Cheryl?

BOBBY: I forgot.

TED: Bobby.

BOBBY: Please.

TED: How long has this been ..?

BOBBY: Like a month I don't know.

TED: Jesus! I love you Bobby you know that but --

BOBBY: Yes, please, stop okay.

TED: -- But you don't even call me?

BOBBY: What am I supposed to say?

TED: Say what's going on. You can't shut your family out
on these things.
What the fuck happened?

BOBBY: He was an unfaithful twoit – that's what happened.

TED: Okay. Well.

BOBBY: Well...?!

TED: That happens.

BOBBY: What do you mean that happens?

TED: You don't think that I with Cheryl – in the beginning
– in the beginning. When we were staying with mom,
Northfield Avenue. I mean Cheryl was big as a house – and
that's no excuse I know but she was MEAN. Fuck I didn't
even know if we were going to stay together. It's like every
little thing I got blamed for. So...

BOBBY: So.

TED: I was just getting beer. And the cashier smiled.

BOBBY: The cashier.

TED: The cashier.

BOBBY: Where the fuck – out back in the parking lot?

TED: No in the Ford – what do you think – Jesus. It was like December.

BOBBY: Before Christmas?

TED: Right she did have that hat on.

BOBBY: You fucked a cashier dressed like an elf in the back of – what CVS?

TED: Walgreens.

BOBBY: Those fuckers! They treat me like a freaking meth head – I'm sneezing and I have to show ID so they can /unlock a case of Zyrtec D?!

TED: /They have to - You've seen Breaking Bad. The whole premise of the show –

BOBBY: TED! So you told Cheryl ...?!

TED: Ah, no, but Cheryl sees all and Cheryl knows all and she just knew I swear to fucking god. Or it was something I wore or I got quiet. Somehow she knew.

That was the worst time of my life. She wouldn't speak for days. For months.

I thought I would die. Because there was just no one else, just ... lonely you know.

And all the while she was so pissed. She got in touch with every one of her skanky high school exs. I saw the emails. "Do you remember that night at French Woods under the stars?"

Please. Drama. Queen.

BOBBY: Peter fucked a girl.

TED: No shit.

BOBBY: I mean where does that put us?

TED: You gotta let it go.

BOBBY: That's a big help coming from Mr. Elf Fucker.

TED: Hey - she was cute.

BOBBY: She was Santa's whore slut demon -- you put your dick inside that.

TED: I can't talk to you like this. You always go to the negative --

BOBBY: I do not –

TED: Yes you do! You have these expectations - but you don't even look around! Accept what is going on that is good – accept when life is good Bobby.

TED: You pull away from people.

BOBBY: Ted.

TED: I'm here for you. I ask you out here because I want you to be a part of things.
It's not easy to have a fucking awesome brother you --

BOBBY: I know! What do you want me to -- ?!

TED: I want you feel for one freaking' moment –what is. I want you to be happy.
You're not the only one who has to work through things!
You think raising Dash is easy?
You do not know. Peter made a mistake but you love Peter. We love Peter. Peter loves you. "I have something to say." We're all just barbequing in the backyard. The guy came out at our house on spring break – for you. The look on his face – him looking at you.

BOBBY: Five years should mean something.

TED: Bobby, five years goes by in the blink of an eye. You can't trust if you can't forgive. Bobby.
You're lucky you have family. I mean -
Peter's dad. In the ER.

BOBBY: What are you talking about?

TED: He didn't tell ...? Peter showed up to see him, I was out smoking. Peter didn't go in. He asked me how his dad was doing. I told him. It's bad Bobby. He came back a few days later.
Still couldn't go in – but he came - with someone.

BOBBY: Someone?

TED: A guy. I thought it was just a --

Beat. Bobby wants to say something else but instead he says:

BOBBY: I'm seeing someone. A kind of someone. And -- I call her.

TED: Who?

BOBBY: The girl he fucked. Nikki.

TED: Why?

BOBBY: I don't know. I don't talk to her. I leave her messages.

TED: What kind of messages? Bobby?

Bobby gently grabs Ted, upset.

BOBBY: *(Trying not to but growing upset)* I don't want Peter here – I don't want you to invite him here - ok?

TED: *(Comforting him)* Alright. Hey. Hey.

Jordy enters.

JORDY: Bobby? *(To Ted)* Heyyyy.

TED: Hi. *(To Bobby)* This is a kind of someone?

BOBBY: Um, Ted. This is --

JORDY: TED! I'm ... I'm Joe.

TED: You've got to go huh?

BOBBY: If that's...

TED: Yeah. I should get back to the hospital. My shift will be starting. Ah the life of an intern.

JORDY: Hey, I'm an intern too. Stocks!

TED: Bodies! Live ones.

JORDY: Cool. Bobby?

BOBBY: I'm still the best man right?

TED: What the fuck is wrong with you - yes! Yes! Always.

Bobby nods. Bobby's phone rings. He looks at – it's Nikki. He lets it ring. We hear her message or she appears delivering the message.

NIKKI: Bobby. *(We hear a cigarette drag)* Bobby. This Saturday. You know where. Nikki.

Immediate blackout.

END OF ACT ONE.

ACT TWO

8. "TRICK"

Saturday. Sound of thunder, drizzly rain. Lights up on Bobby sitting on the bench. Nikki comes in, she has on a hooded jacket, no umbrella. He sees her. They take each other in, size each other up.

NIKKI: Hey.
You are Bobby right.

BOBBY: ...

NIKKI: It stopped drizzling.
It wasn't when I got on the L, then it started.

BOBBY: ....

NIKKI: The whole way over from Lincoln Park.
You can see the storm clouds through the window and that little voice inside me is just going
"What the fuck are you doing Nikki?"
Is this a good idea meeting the fucking psycho leaving messages because you fucked his boyfriend?
Answer: "Nooo...."
Look, I didn't fucking come out to just stand here.

BOBBY: You look different than I expected.

NIKKI: I'm sorry I don't give a shit.

BOBBY: Don't.

NIKKI: What?

BOBBY: Stay over there.

NIKKI: Why?

BOBBY: You stay there, I stay here.

NIKKI: Why?

BOBBY: I don't know it's the way I imagined it.

NIKKI: I do have to work at some point today.

BOBBY: I thought you were a dancer.

NIKKI: I'm not dancing right now.

BOBBY: Gave it up.

NIKKI: Look you – YOU don't get to know about my life –
all you get to do is leave me alone. No more fucking
messages. You do not call me. I don't want to talk to you.
That's all I care about from this conversation. Do you
understand? DO YOU FUCKING UNDERSTAND?

BOBBY: Sometimes you'd stay on the line. I'd hear you
breathing. You came here for the same reason
I'm here. Peter.

NIKKI: I have such great judgment in my life. I fucking love
humanity. I do! If some old lady falls in the street I'm totally
there for her. That's the kind of person I am.

BOBBY: You're helpful.

NIKKI: I'm very fucking helpful. But I will also let that old
bitch know she should be in a scooter and stop wobbling

down the street taking up my fucking time. SO WHAT THE
FUCK DO YOU WANT? What?

BOBBY: Just looking at you.

NIKKI: Why?

BOBBY: I'm trying to picture you on the street. If you'd
walk by, if I just met you. Would I know?

Beat.

Why'd you pick here?

NIKKI: He said you used to come here.

BOBBY: And you just --

NIKKI: I like it here. I like this beach, come here a lot. Way
before –

BOBBY: Where did you come from?

NIKKI: California. Outskirts.

BOBBY: Native.

NIKKI: You stayed.

BOBBY: Yeah.

NIKKI: You stay with him?

BOBBY: ...

NIKKI: The last time I lived with someone he didn't want to go back to London.
I like accents. Being with someone day in and day out I was lucky if I could get out of bed in the morning. It made me depressed. It made me want to sleep until I couldn't wake up. What about you? You like being happy? Or does Peter fill all that for you.

BOBBY: It's none of your fucking business.

NIKKI: He told me you were unhappy with him. You sure you haven't had adventures of your own?

BOBBY: Shut up.

NIKKI: Oh. You don't like being a slut like me.

BOBBY: I didn't say you were a slut.

NIKKI: You want me to hit replay?

BOBBY: Maybe I did.

NIKKI: Well I'm so fucking glad we got that out of the way.

BOBBY: And I didn't mean slut like -- I'm a very progressive person. My mother raised me on Gloria Steinem, Ms. Magazine, Maya Angelou --

NIKKI: Just fucking stop for a second okay?

BOBBY: Don't fucking tell me --

Nikki does a dance move that totally makes Bobby shut up and just stare at her. He impulsively mimics her. This goes on as long as needed until they break, laughing a little.

NIKKI: I can tell. Seriously. God. But you've got some grace. You'd be a good fuck.

BOBBY: What?

NIKKI: If you move with grace you're a good fuck. Is that ok with you?

BOBBY: Jesus. He didn't tell me you were insane.

NIKKI: Well I am. I'm horribly fucking insane. What did he tell you?

BOBBY: You were a mistake.

NIKKI: Fuck you.

BOBBY: Your life is a mistake.

NIKKI: My life has nothing to do with you.

BOBBY: Nothing to do with me?

NIKKI: Screaming into the phone "You are not going to ruin years of love?" Like I can do that – who says that?!

BOBBY: I wasn't screaming.

NIKKI: YEARS OF LOVE! Only you deserve that – just you? Not anybody else.

BOBBY: WE WERE FINE. /We were fine until you--.

NIKKI: No, no, no most likely – most likely - it was EASY - easy until me --even a stranger could see something was wrong/ --

BOBBY: No you - you don't know --

NIKKI: -- I know you want to pretend – I know – ok? Ok. So pretend. Pretend you had one bad night. Pretend he did. That I --. That I am a truly horrible person. I'm going home. You should too.

Nikki turns to go.

BOBBY: There was something wrong. You were right. Peter was right. I was pulling away. I love the shit out of him but – we eat on the porch with my family, we walk down the street and – it's becoming familiar. Like we are the same. Like I'm disappearing. In that instinct to live inside him, to want our lives together – I'm lost.
I'm losing myself, my pride, my just whoever the fuck I am-I just want one night to be again. To feel –

NIKKI: It's over ok? One night. One stupid--.

BOBBY: Could you tell?

NIKKI: Tell?

BOBBY: He loved someone like me.

NIKKI: Who cares?

BOBBY: I care.

NIKKI: You're the one he's with. He's with you. You're together. You have something.

BOBBY: It's killing me because every time I close my eyes I see you. You were with him and then the world opened up, the world changed. I need to know – just to know. And maybe I can ... One shred of honesty. Truth. Do you understand?

Beat, Nikki takes this in.

NIKKI: We came here after the bar. I asked if he was with someone. He said yes.
I asked, "How long?" He wouldn't say.
We did shots. He had ecstasy.

BOBBY: Fuck.

NIKKI: He told me your name was Bobby. I told him I didn't care. I mean I told him I fucked women before, that's true.

BOBBY: And ...?

NIKKI: And. You really ...?

Bobby nods.

NIKKI: It was quick. But good. I'm sorry.
Honest to god.
But it was ...
It shouldn't mean anything, right?

BOBBY: Then why did you call me back?
What did you call that day to tell him?
What did you come here today to tell me?

She doesn't answer. It starts to rain. Bobby puts up his umbrella. Nikki pulls sweatshirt around her.

BOBBY: You didn't bring anything. You're going to get a cold.

NIKKI: You care?

BOBBY: I'm fucking human, yes.

NIKKI: It's hot out. It's a hot rain.

BOBBY: I don't care. Come here. Come under here.

Bobby goes to her, holding the umbrella up covering the two of them standing very close now. Nikki looks up at Bobby.

NIKKI: When I called Peter. I was at the doctor's.

BOBBY: ...

NIKKI: Before you met him. Did you ever imagine love?
I close my eyes and I do.
I see.
So many things.
A house. A yard. Someone, someone.
The people all around you knowing you're in love.

BOBBY: ...

NIKKI: It doesn't matter what he would have said. I just thought.
I thought someone should know.

BOBBY: ...
Nikki.

NIKKI: I like the way you say my name. Even when he wouldn't let me say his –
Love is...wild. I pretended that night it was...

BOBBY: You felt like it was--

NIKKI: I always feel that way. I always let myself feel that way. That's the trick.

Bobby holds her. She lets him. We transition. Phone ringing.

PETER: You've reached Peter Marks. Leave a message.

Beep.

VIN: Bleep! Peter I got your text. Sunrise. I'll be there. Peettterrr...

9. "THIS"

Next morning. Just before sunrise. Lights up on Peter and Vin. Vin shows Peter yoga moves.

PETER: Wow. I can't believe you do this every morning - amazing -

VIN: Watch me. Do what I do.

Vin does a yoga move.

PETER: Wow. What is that --?

VIN: The cobra.

PETER: Yeah. And the point of all this again is –

VIN: Breathe Peter.

PETER: I am.

VIN: You seriously need to focus if you want me to make you flexible.

PETER: I'm very flexible.

VIN: You walk as if every bone in your body is clenched.

PETER: Ah, so wise zen master.

VIN: In Brooklyn at 4 am we used to practice on the roof.

PETER: In the suburbs we used to sleep. But look I'm up now.

VIN: Uh-huh.

PETER: What's this?

VIN: Downward dog.

PETER: So... Bobby.

VIN: How is he? Breathe.

PETER: Bobby. He came home the other day ... I've never seen him like that. I ask him what's wrong.
He won't tell me.

VIN: What do you think is wrong?

PETER: I don't know. I like this. Don't you.

VIN: I do.

PETER: I love doing this. Being flexible. I like being here with you. The *(gestures out)* waves and shit.

VIN: Good.

PETER: You never talk about anyone else.

VIN: Why so many questions?

PETER: I don't know.

VIN: Okay.

PETER: You texted back right away last night. You were up late. Where were you?

VIN: I met a friend.

PETER: Where did you go?

VIN: Peter.

PETER: Right. Why is it so dark?

VIN: It's because it's early. That's why people come out to watch the sunrise.

PETER: Let's watch it, then. Let's watch the sunrise.

VIN: I don't want to disappoint you Peter.

PETER: Why would you disappoint me?

VIN: It's just been a few weeks and I know this is when it gets into this.

PETER: What's this?

VIN: Questions.

PETER: I like questions.

VIN: So do I. I'm just saying don't expect answers.

PETER: Okay. But...

VIN: Let it go.

PETER: Maybe Zen Master should tell me what he's feeling.

VIN: Let it go --

PETER: I am.

VIN: Let it go --

PETER: I am letting go - of all of it.

VIN: Everything but Bobby.

PETER: You're angry.

VIN: No.

PETER: You can be angry Zen Master. You can raise your voice.

VIN: No.

PETER: Yes.

VIN: I don't NEED to act that way.

PETER: Well people do, you know. People act that way all the time.

VIN: AND WHY DO YOU WANT ME TO ACT THAT WAY? THIS IS HOW YOU WANT TO DEFINE THINGS? LIKE THIS -- LIKE --

Peter starts making out with Vin.

PETER: This. This is great, this is what I look forward to.

Peter and Vin are going at it pretty heavy.

I touch you and I make you forever. This is forever.

VIN: Nothing is forever.

Peter starts jerking Vin off.

PETER: You are. I'll make you that.

VIN: Why?

PETER: Because you're –

VIN: Why do you always have to be in control?

Vin stops Peter, starts jerking Peter off. For the first Peter lets this happen.

PETER: When I leave you, I leave you here, I walk into Mesirow – Clients screaming: "I don't want to lose! I don't want to be a loser! Help me win!" And I scream back: "Technology! Green Mountain Coffee! Emerging markets with long lasting value" and I come home, try to sleep, him next to me but not next to me, but I'm slipping away! I'm falling because every part of you is kind. Every part of you gives, I know it and I want to hold that – I want to make it into me. I want to become you until I disappear --

Peter totally surrenders to Vin, climaxes. Beat.

VIN: Last night. I met my friend. And he orders what we used to drink and I don't say no. Because he's kind. Because we were together once. Or just because. We go back to his hotel room on Michigan Ave. We check out porn, we call up someone. And we do this – this because he wants to, because I want to. Because I feel expectations, years of expectations - of this and this and -.. My friend I saw last night. I care about so many things. No one just gives love. No matter how hard we try – we expect. No one lets us just be. You want to define us because you can't define what you have with Bobby.

PETER: And you can't admit you deserve - You deserve love, Vin.

VIN: But I fuck it up.

PETER: Wow.

VIN: Are you happy now?

PETER: You're human.

VIN: Yeah. Very human. With my friend. With anyone.
Love? No one knows. No one ever knows.
Not when it's happening. Not like they should.

PETER: You feel shitty.

VIN: Yes.

PETER: I feel shitty. So let's not pretend. Whoever you were
with last night doesn't matter. I care that you care. I care
about you. Be with me. I'll be whatever you need.

Peter and Vin go at it again, undressing each other.

VIN: Peter --

PETER: I don't want to ruin this. I like falling asleep
holding you, I like people watching us as we kiss, I like
going under the waves with you when it rains. I love you
Bobby.

*Vin looks at Peter, half naked, in front of him having said
Bobby's name more naturally than anything in the world.
Vin gathers his things.*

VIN: If you do let yourself - if you let yourself love someone
you don't make them who they are.
You let them. Be.

*Vin kisses Peter on the forehead, goes. Peter is alone on the
beach. He looks up – the sun is rising.*

10. "BREAK"

In transition, ringing, voicemail picks up.

PETER: You've reached Peter Marks. Leave a message.

Beep.

TED: Peter. Peter. It's Ted. Please. Call me back. It's about your dad.

Lights up on Peter and Ted on the beach very late at night.

TED: I don't know how you take it.

PETER: It's okay.

TED: They've had me on this shift for the last week, yeah. It makes me loopy.

PETER: Okay.

Ted peers at Peter who seems to be acting as if everything's just fine.

TED: Wow, you're taking this very ... It's a lot to go up there and...
I see a lot of - loved ones – they come by to see a parent – a father looking like that and they have some kind of --

PETER: They cry.

TED: Some kind of emotional response, yes.

Beat. Ted isn't sure what to say - starts eating junk food.

PETER: Huh. I didn't know you were such a ... chunky monkey.

TED: You want some? Snickers, M&Ms, Poptarts. You know stuff to wake me up, keep going. I go 'til 8 AM.

PETER: That's crazy.

TED: Bobby would have wanted you to wake him up.

PETER: Bobby won't talk to me, he won't tell me what's wrong. This morning ... after ... I go to work. Bobby's not there. Called in sick today. Everyone asking where he is. I go home – just walk out of work and go home and he won't look at me.

TED: Aren't you...

PETER: Worried sick, yes of course I am don't you think --

TED: I think you should be aware - a little aware of your actions – how they affect him – yeah.

PETER: I am trying to be --

TED: You love each other. You stay together for a reason. He loves you for a reason. You love him for a reason. Show him that.

PETER: Your brother, wakes up one morning - he starts pulling away. And all I want is one person to let me in. I find it with her. One moment that's all it was. I don't know how to take it away.
The more we try the more we make it complicated and we end up here.

TED: You want complicated? Cheryl ... I go home to a
woman trying to stitch fucking tulle and Cheryl can NOT
sew a fucking button -- it's all "did you do anything from
the big wedding board chart" and my kid will not sleep until
I make something up about a bunny on fire.

PETER: I love Dash. He's amazing.

TED: He is amazing.

PETER: Dad of the year. That's what I think Bobby wants.
Everything you have.

TED: So?

PETER: That scares the shit out of me. Bobby showed me
this spot. He brings other people here now.
All summer.

TED: The same place? Here? THAT'S – I'm sorry – that's –
that's bullshit.

PETER: I brought her here.

TED: Jesus. You think you could - try a little fucking
harder?!

PETER: I'm trying. I'm evolving.

TED: Into what? You don't think I stare at Cheryl at like six
in the morning when I get home from shifts - wonder where
she's been out all night? Even the thought of her – you can't
even imagine what it does to me.

PETER: I'm sorry Ted – but this has been a really fucked up
night and I don't need –

TED: Everyone feels a little fucking unloved now and then and everybody needs!
You don't see what you have, you lose it. You lose it and it doesn't come back.
I hear the nurses say your last name. Your sister wanting to take your dad off support.
I bring you in tonight – up the elevator to your dad's room. This. This is the last night you'll have with him. Tomorrow he'll be gone but tonight you didn't have to walk in alone. You were not alone tonight. That is family. That is fucking family do you know that?

PETER: Ted.

TED: I'm sorry, I'm sorry. But I'm here. You hurt my brother. But I'm here and you --

PETER: *(Outburst)* I lost Bobby! I love him. I love him and I don't know what to do ... Ted.

TED: I come home last night and Cheryl – she's gone – she's not even fucking there. My heart is racing. And then I hear something from the backyard steps. I come out and she's just looking down all the wooden steps, into the backyard downstairs, looking at the garden. She just looks up and her face just -. "I miss you." And I hug her. I hold her. I just --. Everyone in love, every parent lives with something like that in their heart because they have known somebody they can't let go. I don't let it eat away at me. I love. I love you. I love Bobby. You made a mistake. I live with mine every day. You want him to forgive you – but you can't yourself. And you have to. If you love him. That's what you do when you love. You give. You have to.
That's why I called you. That's why I'm here.

Ted goes and hugs Peter.

I'm your fucking brother. Love. That stays. You fucked up –
we fuck up but we ...you being part of our family. That
stays.
And if somewhere in you - you can realize why you fucked
up ... that ... that's what makes the ones you love come
back. But you have to accept them.
Since I told him Bobby has been out to see your dad every
night. Stayed with him sometimes.
These past few days, when he didn't come by I should have
known something was but with the wedding I ...
You should-.
Gotta go back.

Singing the Beastie Boys song:

"No sleep 'til ... Northwestern Memorial Hospital!"

PETER: My dad.

TED: When they get taken off support. It takes some time
once they've been taken off. About a day.

PETER: You'll stay with him right.

TED: I will.

PETER: And that's it.

TED: That's it.

PETER: That's how I say goodbye.

TED: That's how sometimes. You...?

Peter is almost crying, nods, recovers.

PETER: Just a few weeks until the wedding.

TED: It scares the hell out of me.

PETER: Why?

TED: I love her.

We transition into the following voicemail:

BOBBY: Hello you've reached Robert (Bobby) Lahman, Junior Client Reporting Associate at Mesirow Financial. Please leave a message and I'll get back to you as soon as I can.

Beep. Jordy speaks over the background noise of a party.

Jordy: Hey Bobby – I got your message - you want to meet me? *(To others)* Shut up! *(Into phone)* I'm coming now. BYYYYEEE.

11. "MESSAGE"

That night on the beach. Jordy comes, buries something in the sand. Bobby enters.

BOBBY: Jordy --

JORDY: Out with it. You missed me.

BOBBY: Jordy.

JORDY: You did. I knew it.
You look awful.

BOBBY: Have you seen Peter?

JORDY: You're looking for him.

BOBBY: It's important.

JORDY: He wasn't at work. He wasn't at the party.

BOBBY: What --?

JORDY: My party. Paddys ... It's my last day Bobby.

BOBBY: Right ... It's your last ... I'm sorry I forgot ...

JORDY: Everyone else remembered. Everyone is sad to see me go. But you know ... at least I didn't get canned ... I ... lasted! The whole summer. It's been...

BOBBY: Jordy.

JORDY: I don't know where Peter is.

BOBBY: The way I've been acting ... it has nothing to do with you.

JORDY: Really is that why you blew me off?

BOBBY: I shouldn't have started anything - it wasn't fair.

JORDY: What isn't fair is it's my last day. I'm supposed to be going back tomorrow. Kansas. I thought we might want to ...

BOBBY: No.

JORDY: Is that why you stopped going to work all week.

BOBBY: No. I met her.

JORDY: Who?

BOBBY: The girl. The one Peter ... It changed things.

JORDY: Because you care about Peter.

BOBBY: I'm worried. My brother called me and he told me-

JORDY: What?

BOBBY: It's family stuff.

JORDY: I buried it.

BOBBY: What are you talking about?

JORDY: Something for you. Something really special for you. You have to find it.
You can start anywhere. It's like a hunt. In the sand.

BOBBY: I get that --

JORDY: Look. I'm helping. I'm helping make it go faster.

BOBBY: Jordy.

Jordy kisses him.

BOBBY: What are you on.

JORDY: I think you need some. I think you need a lot.

BOBBY: Look just take it easy and --

JORDY: I've been going out.

BOBBY: Good. You should keep going out and meet people I told you.

JORDY: It was so incredible. A couple at the lounge. We all went into this big fancy bathroom. It was great so why I wake up thinking of you I have no idea. We all fuck for different reasons. You fucked me to get back at Peter.

BOBBY: Not just that.

JORDY: Not just that but you did - yes. Say it!

BOBBY: Yes.

JORDY: Yes! Right, it's complicated. And I do everything in the office, everything for you, take care of you, I'm there for you at night.

BOBBY: You're better than me. You deserve better than me.

JORDY: Like Peter? With that slut.

BOBBY: She's not a slut.

JORDY: I am. Because I fucked you and you still love him - Peter - his dumb dress shoes – his everything - he's --

BOBBY: I am sorry - I am sorry - I am ---

JORDY: You have family. You're his family. What do I have?

BOBBY: You'll find it. I promise you. Just please. He must be at the office. He must be somewhere --

JORDY: Mesirow? Peter wouldn't be there. And if he was at the party. If he was no one would talk to him.

BOBBY: Why?

JORDY: You think there's a place for you there?

Beat.

BOBBY: What does that...?

JORDY: You know I don't want to go back.

BOBBY: Jordy –

JORDY: You're not looking for your present.

Jordy kicks up the sand.

That's it. It's right there.

Bobby picks it up.

It's a message. In a bottle.

Bobby opens the bottle and pulls out the piece of paper inside. He reads, not believing what he's reading, but it's setting in.

JORDY: The firing list from the board meetings. I swiped it. That's it. You're on it. It's you. You and Peter. They'll do it right before the weekend. Before the vacation. I told them but they've known about you both in the office. Just needed an excuse and since you started calling in sick -. Peter not coming in today. They know you've been together. They see how you look at each other.

BOBBY: Shut up.

JORDY: No one has to worry about it anymore. I told them. I told them. So ... get pissed ... get angry. C'mon. C'MON!!

Beat. Bobby is fuming. He goes up to Jordy. Beat. He breaths, calms down.

BOBBY: I'm sorry. I'm so --

Jordy punches Bobby. Bobby feels his mouth, he's bleeding. Jordy takes a box cutter out of his pocket.

JORDY: I'm not going home.

BOBBY: Jordy.

JORDY: I don't want to go back home.

BOBBY: You don't have to – you don't have to do anything you don't want to –

JORDY: You never want anything from anyone. But you expect. You expect the world. No one can give you that. I'm going to...right here.

Bobby rushes Jordy and grabs the box cutter away from him.

BOBBY: Go home. Go home Jordy.

Jordy goes off. Bobby is alone. Bobby is losing it.

BOBBY:
Try.
Try.
Try.
Let...

Bobby breaks down. Peter enters.

PETER: Bobby.

Bobby looks up at Peter on the verge of tears. Peter goes to him. Bobby clutches him tight. While holding onto each other:

BOBBY: We're fired.

Beat.

PETER: Good.

BOBBY: Good?

PETER: Good.

BOBBY: Your dad...

PETER: I know.

BOBBY: Nikki.

PETER: You met her. She texted me.

BOBBY: What did she say?

PETER: *(Looking right at Bobby)* That you're amazi

BOBBY: She was pregnant. That's why she called.

PETER: I didn't...

BOBBY: She let it go and the kicker is I imagine all this time - us - a family – having our own – God -- all the thoughts I never tell you because I look at you and I love you but I'm --

PETER: We. We are.

BOBBY: ...

PETER: We just fucking are.

BOBBY: Peter, I'm scared.

PETER: I walked. Every place you ever showed me. The whole city, the sidewalks, the parks, along the water, the --. I don't know how long. I just keep going, the sun keeps rising and I keep walking the entire city ... our city. Everything. Us. in every building, light and street. I walk every piece of myself back to you and for the first time in months I feel like Peter. I can call myself Peter. I go home and you're not there. I need you here Bobby. That night - whatever it was with her. After we ... I kept looking at her body here. Heard the waves and when I closed my eyes, when I touched her - her body was your body. You. Our first night. Here. I transferred in and some sophomore kid named Bobby said "Follow me, follow me" and we --

BOBBY: We ran.

PETER: We ran. Hopped on the L and the streets got smaller and smaller and I couldn't imagine. In a city. The

waves. "I love water," he said. "I love watching the waves."
But I wouldn't let him watch. We jumped in. Bobby.

BOBBY: "Love is wild."

*Peter smiles. They are serious but playfulness is creeping
back in, as they once were. Peter kisses Bobby. Bobby kisses
back then lightly slaps Peter, Peter pulls him in. While
kissing and talking:*

PETER: When I go you think of me. Wild thoughts.

BOBBY: Fuck you.

PETER: Fuck you.
I know you do.
You're thinking of me.

Kiss.

Why?

Kiss.

Why?

Kiss.

BOBBY: Why?

*Bobby smiles, genuine, real, free. He kisses Peter ever so
gently. Sound of the waves. Music up.*

BLACKOUT. End of play.

Welcome to the Now Now was developed by Middle Voice at Rattlestick Playwrights Theatre. A reading was presented by Missing Bolts Productions (Blair Baker and Zac Kline, Artistic Directors) and NoPassport Theatre on November 13th, 2016 at DR2 in New York City.

Welcome to the Now Now

A play by Crystal Skillman
from *After Orlando, an International Theatre Action
response to the Pulse Nightclub Shooting*

*Lights bump up on Olivia, 21, in her bedroom. Huge
Skullcandy headphones. She is recording a podcast.*

OLIVIA: Ladybugs. Cats. Small cats. Large cats. Bunnies.
And…

A spotlight appears revealing…

OLIVIA: My best friend and co-host Greer. Greer?

*Greer, 25, smiles. He is in his room getting dressed talking
on a headset. He is dressing up. He looks good!*

GREER: Yup, I hear you—

OLIVIA: We have a good connection!

GREER: Skype's on fire today. But rabbits, seriously Olivia?
Mom didn't let us have pets.

OLIVIA: They make me smile. And now is the point in our
podcast for "1,000 Million Things That Make Me Smile and
I Tell You Why" where I'll tell you 1,000 million things that
make me smile and I tell you why. This is the part where we
list!

GREER: You love lists!

OLIVIA: I do!

GREER: I love you, man.

OLIVIA: Well, if I mean so much to you, you wouldn't be phoning in on the 50th episode of our podcast that we lovingly started together, am I right?

GREER: Uh-huh, and if you really cared about this podcasting stuff, you'd actually post the stuff we record.

OLIVIA: I don't need communications advice, okay?

GREER: It is my major. You got this idea from me!

OLIVIA: Uh-huh. You've been going to CUNY for six years. When do you graduate again?

GREER: Listen, Ms. Fancy Iowa writing program—

OLIVIA: SMILE. What tops your "Millionth Smile" list today, Greer?

Beat.

GREER: I love our podcast!

OLIVIA: Me too!!

GREER: But you know...Olivia. Every band knows when their last song was played.

OLIVIA: What...?

GREER: Well...it's kinda been getting stale, and you don't really take chances, Olivia. I mean we could do anything, but lately all you want is to just sit and do this in your room all day...and life is short, you know—

OLIVIA: You don't know me.

GREER: I'm your brother.

OLIVIA: Yeah, I doubt we're even from the same inserted semen.

GREER: We're family. I worry about you.

OLIVIA: Really? You never come visit.

GREER: Well, you never come home. Ever since you got dumped, you've been like—

OLIVIA: Don't say it—

GREER: Like some kind of sulky hermit.

OLIVIA: HEY!! I am a wild son of a bitch, okay?

GREER: Grant and I are starting one. Our own podcast.

OLIVIA Grant? 'Flavor of the month' Grant? When?

GREER: Now?

OLIVIA: Now now?

GREER: Welcome, to the Now Now, yes. Grant and I are recording in like a minute now now. Olivia? This is my last show with you, but we're forever, we're family—

OLIVIA: NEVER. NEVER AM I EVER GOING TO STOP HATING YOU. I'm shitballs insanely pissed with you and that is not going away. You are not even in the room and I don't feel loved. I don't feel love HEARING YOUR

FUCKING VOICE—

GREER: Shit, you're making me sound—

OLIVIA: No one is making you sound. No one cares what you sound like. No one cares about you and your ass voice!! I'm glad this is all being recorded!

GREER: You're really going to keep taping. This is the one you're going to finally post?

OLIVIA: Fuck yeah I am! I came up with this show and I don't edit. I don't censor like some kind of Nazi. I don't cry when I find out my best friend is starting a podcast with his month old boyfriend. I don't cry. This podcast is called *1,000 Million Things That Make Me Smile and I'll Tell You Why.* And I'm going to keep smiling WITHOUT YOU.

Greer hangs up. Olivia fumes in her light. She finds a cool hat in her room, puts it on and dances around. Greer collects himself and sets up his podcast.

OLIVIA: FUCKING SMILING. STAY WITH ME HERE FOLKS!

GREER: *(Flustered)* Okay, Okay.

Olivia plays a punk song. Greer plays a punk song. It's the same song.

GREER: Hello, world! This is my new podcast. *Greer and Grant and the Songs that Changed your Life.*

The door bursts open in Greer's space. Grant, 27, is there. He wears sunglasses and a porkpie hat and has a guitar

slung across his back. In his mind, he looks like a badass.
He is always humming/playing something.

OLIVIA: Hey!

GREER: Grant!

GRANT: You're not mad I'm late. You're happy I'm here.

OLIVIA: *(Podcasting)* I used to never smile. I was the girl
you'd pass in the street and I looked like I was going to kick
your teeth in.

GREER: You could get here on time.

GRANT: We could do this anytime. It's a podcast. You
choose when you record.

OLIVIA Bah! Bah! Bah! I didn't care!

GREER: Except in the Doodle survey monkey of our
relationship you said 9:45 PM on the weekend was the only
time you had available.

GRANT: Let's sing. Let's fucking sing.

OLIVIA But then it got out that I was dating Terra, I was a
walking huge toothy grin and the whole campus was like--
Olivia! She's that girl.

GREER: So what song are we going to play for our
listeners? Grant!

OLIVIA Terra. GRRRR. I hope you're happy you dumped
me. I hope you hear this, Terra. I hope you hear this next to
whoever you're partying with and I upload this and I hope
you FEEL LIKE THE FUCK HEAD YOU ARE!

GRANT: Yes! I was thinking *[actor suggests song]*.

Greer responds by singing something totally opposite of that song. Grant and Greer kiss.

OLIVIA: Who dumps someone in the summer? It's like when you get a cold and all you want to do is go outside to the park, but you're puking your guts out. It's unnatural.

GRANT: Okay. What is it about that song, right?

GREER: What is there to talk about? It's all there in the song. But our podcast is talking about how the song we share makes us feel...personal memories. Deconstructing how we feel.

GRANT: I hear that song in my mind when I cross a parking lot. At night. And I need the courage to live in this city.

GREER: I thought you were a badass.

GRANT: I am a badass. And a badass shares their feelings.

They kiss again.

GRANT: Mmm.

GREER: Kissing! We're kissing. I don't know if they know that. Oh, I know the next song!

Grant plays/hums the Beatles "A Day in the Life". Geer lays down a beat. They can also play this on their Iphone.

OLIVIA: Grant is a pompous weirdo. My brother was always seduced by guys who play music. Correction: Guys who try to play music. I have a band. Okay, sometimes I play guitar -

just me - a few cords, it is not tuned. But I do it at
Dougan's, the late night bar in town, on Open Mic night.
It's pretty empty there and it's depressing and it has darts
and I don't know, I like it, so maybe that's why I go. Maybe
that's why I go and play badly. And I see...her. This girl. She
was in the band setting up after the Open Mic night. A real
band. She goes up to get a drink before the set. She was
drinking and...I don't go around looking for people, ok? But
I drink and I walk around looking at all the seats that are
filled with folks drinking, not even caring, and all of a
sudden she's there and I've got to go. And she grabs my
arm. Lightly, but. She doesn't even fucking know me.
"Aren't you gonna stay for the second set?!" I look up and
she leans in, no joke: "Hey my music is gonna change your
heart. My music is going to change your soul." If Greer were
here he would have said: "She said that?" YES SHE
FUCKING SAID THAT, GREER. It was in her eyes. There
was- it was -don't laugh - like a cliche in a song - swear to
god - there were like wild horses in her eyes. Yeah, yeah.
There was. Pulling, pushing. There was just something
about her. There was some deep instinct you know that this
green eyed - yeah she had green eyes - but this instinct that
- this - this was love. If Greer were here he'd say: "What did
you do?" And I'd say "listen! Greer! My brother! You are
supposed to be my family, so for once in your life listen."
And Terra came, this was about a week before she dumps
me ("I'm too serious, I'm too lame, I'm whatever") but this
one night - when the wild horses woman of my dreams is
there. Terra goes home early. She's got exams. She's okay if
I stay. That green eyed woman ... This woman just smiled.
She got up and played. And you know what I did? And no
one does this at Dougans because it's lame so lame - no one
ever does - but I danced. I danced right there in Dougans
where no one dances because no one would be caught dead
doing that at Dougans. She played. And she came down
after one song and we were dancing. We were drunk. And at

some point I turned. At some point she's gone. I go home to my dorm and try to sleep but it's like there's wild horses in me, pulling me and I wake up and I... where am I ever going to find love like that? I didn't get her number. I don't know where the fuck she is. I don't know where love is. Three months later Terra breaks up with me. I look for a way to keep smiling. I start this podcast with my brother. I miss him. I make these. I don't post them. I want some kind of answer but what's the question?

GREER/GRANT *(to "A Day in the Life")*
I'D LOVE TO TURN YOU ON

Intense sound of shooting. Bombs. Orlando. "Day in the Life" climaxes at the end, building and building. Greer, Grant and Olivia look out and are very still. The music cuts out. The text below is spoken or can just be projected.

Where was the bomb?
Where was the shooting?
Another one?
Was it somewhere else?
Was it here?
Was it me?
Was it you?

OLIVIA: The world stops. I think about the woman with green eyes. I think about her. I forget the drunk guy talking with his friends I passed by putting on my jacket. On the way out. You think old? 24. He goes to my school. I remember the girl with green eyes - I forget what I hear him say: "You can be trans, you can be gay, you can be whatever, you have that right - this is America, I just don't want to see it. I don't want it in front of me. I don't want to see it. Don't do it. Don't be it. Don't live in front of me." And here's what makes me cry: Did I forget that because I want to, because I want to bury it inside, or because I hear it every day? Smile...smile. I try.

They stand there. Each starts to move slightly. There is a musicality to it. We begin to realize it's Sly and the Family Stones' "Everybody is a Star", which someone starts playing on their Iphone. Perhaps even all three are playing that song, slightly behind. Each in their space, they are dancing, but they are connected. Near the end of it, Grant takes off his sunglasses. He puts on regular glasses. He takes off his pork pie hat and puts on a 7/11 cap. He puts on an apron. He is now totally uncool, but lovely.

GRANT: I gotta go. Night Shift. You okay?

GREER: Yeah.

Grant smiles. He does a little impressive dance for Greer. Greer smiles. Grant kisses Greer. Grant exits. Beat. Greer calls Olivia. Olivia sees who is calling. She picks up.

OLIVIA: Greer! Greer. You fucking hear...? The news?

GREER: How you doing baby?

Beat.

GREER: I'm sorry. You're still recording?

OLIVIA: Yeah. You?

Greer cries. Olivia has never heard her brother cry before. It sounds strange to her.

OLIVIA: Hey, are you...?

GREER: You are gonna find love, baby. You are so, so, so gonna find love.

OLIVIA: How's your show?

GREER: Uh, I don't know. I like Grant. Look, I'm getting a plane ticket. This weekend. I'm coming to visit. Fucking Iowa, Jesus.

OLIVIA: Greer. I don't want to stop recording. I don't want to ever stop...

GREER: I know.

OLIVIA: Can I sing you something?

GREER: Yeah.

OLIVIA: I'm not a singer.

GREER: I know.

OLIVIA: I can only play a few cords.

GREER: I know.

Olivia takes her guitar. She sings her song.

OLIVIA:
BRO, YOUR MUSIC IS GONNA CHANGE MY HEART MY
MUSIC IS GONNA SAVE YOUR SOUL LOVE'S WILD
HORSES PUSH ME, STOP/START WE LET THE WORLD
SEE US WE MAKE THE WORLD WHOLE

GREER: That's the end of the Smile episode.

OLIVIA: Yeah...I just changed the name.

GREER: Post it, Olivia.

OLIVIA: Goodnight, Greer.

End of play.

ABOUT THE PLAYWRIGHT

Crystal Skillman is the award-winning author of the plays *Geek, Cut*, and *King Kirby* (co-written with Fred Van Lente), all Critic's Picks from the *NY Times*. She is the musical theater book writer of *Mary and Max* (based on the film) written with award-winning ASCAP Composer/Lyricist Bobby Cronin. Her new plays include: *Rain and Zoe Save the World* (2016 New Harmony Project, 2016 Oregon Performance Lab), *Pulp Vérité* (2015 Clifford Odets Ensemble Play Commission, 2016 BAPF Finalist) and *Open* (All for One Solo Theater Company's 2016 Season) as well as *Another Kind of Love, a punk rock play* (Chopin Theater with InFusion Theatre Co., 2015, Chicago) hailed by the *Chicago Reader* as a "Masterpiece". Awards include two Ensemble Studio Theater/Sloan commissions, as well as the New York Innovation Award for Outstanding Full Length Play (*The Vigil or the Guided Cradle*). Her work has been featured as part of MCC Theater's Playwrights' Coalition, Women's Project Playwrights' Lab, Soho Rep Writer/Director Lab, the Lark, and New Georges. Crystal is represented by UTA. www.CrystalSkillman.com

Printed in Great Britain
by Amazon

76750529R00056